'Sharp, bright and inq[...]
— Rachel Long, auth[...]

'An intimately render[...]
territories of playgrou[...]
streets. Language is deftly deboned here, laid bare like a
scraped knee, into poems of wondrous observation.'
— Momtaza Mehri, author of *Doing the Most with the Least*

'Sarah's poetry is its own incandescent truth—tangible and
expansive, tender and scalpel-sharp, giddying and unafraid.
With an unassuming yet unmistakable sure-footedness in
each deft step, this is a body of work to be admired.'
— Jacob Sam-La Rose, author of *Breaking Silence*

'I love these poems, so startling in their capacity for deep
attention; each one so vividly alight as though possessed of
its own life. *Fovea / Ages Ago* is a radiant debut from Sarah
Lasoye. Her vision is sharp. Her voice is glisteningly clear.'
— Victoria Adukwei Bulley, author of *Girl B*

'Sarah Lasoye's unwavering poetic voice guides us
through a delicate journey of coming to know oneself.
Written with joy and intention, every poem is as perfectly
sculpted as the one before it. A gorgeous debut that will
stay with you long after reading.'
— Hibaq Osman, author of *where the memory was*

'*Fovea / Ages Ago* is in every sense a visionary debut—a
collection of prismatic, Time-traced lyrics where memory
and matter braid together and where muscle and image,
clarity and mystery are kith and kin.'
— R. A. Villanueva, author of *Reliquaria*

FOVEA / AGES AGO

First published in the United Kingdom in 2021
by Hajar Press C.I.C.
www.hajarpress.com
@hajarpress

© Sarah Lasoye, 2021

ISBN 978-1-914221-00-2 Paperback
ISBN 978-1-914221-06-4 EPUB eBook

A Cataloguing-in-Publication data record for this book is available
from the British Library.

Extract from 'Poem for My Love' by June Jordan, *Directed by Desire:
The Collected Poems of June Jordan*, edited by Sara Miles and Jan
Heller Levi, Copper Canyon Press, 2005. © 2005, 2021, June M. Jordan
Literary Estate Trust. Used by permission. www.junejordan.com

Cover and interior art: Hanna Stephens
Cover design: Samara Jundi
Typesetting: Laura Jones / lauraflojo.com

Printed and bound in the United Kingdom by
Clays Ltd, Elcograf S.p.A.

FOVEA / AGES AGO

SARAH LASOYE

Contents

AUTHOR'S NOTE

Primary school was, is still, the most sweet, sour, tender, sore time of my life. The memories of each first-feeling are still clear as day. I can tell you about the first time I swore at another kid, that first delightful feeling of freed spite (I had broken my thumb, my arm was in a sling, and he wouldn't let me play football), or the first time I felt guilt (caught throwing some fish fillets from my school dinner under the lunch table), or the first time I felt *real* guilt (caught giving money to my best friend, having blamed my brother for the two disappearing £10 notes), or the first time I felt a kind of guilt-flavoured shame (promising Miss Owen I could swim, begging not to be put in the beginners group, then gasping, walking back the quarter-length of the pool, chlorine at the back of my throat). On reflection, there was a lot of guilt, and usually as the direct result of a lie.

One thing no one ever seems to expect is that I was a compulsive liar as a kid, or perhaps an impulsive one. These days I'm more careful about what I share—still open, but mindful and deliberate. As a child, I lied about meaningless things, impossible but harmless lies, inoffensive and credible—like, my cousin met someone from the *Misfits* cast—whose consequences I knew would entrap me but, always being quite simple to forget, left me undeterred. A lost night's sleep, one of those ugly cries only children can summon, and maybe, if needed, a second white lie to repair any loss in social standing. Back then, I would be able to convince myself—wholly and entirely—that these lies were true. It was a particular commitment to self-delusion that I now find deeply worrying and mildly admirable. It'd be a fun exercise to think of it as a kind of 'world-making', a precursor to the kind of radical imagination I'm now committed to cultivating. That, of course, would be untrue too—but it'd be funny to think about it like that, so humour me for a second.

When you're a kid, the world is fixed in a way so beyond your control you don't even notice it. You are moving your mouth and there is sound coming out—a sound you are told is your voice—and most of the time you are only really making this sound in response to something that already has a world-fixed answer. But when you lie, you splinter off somewhere else, and you're not just moving your mouth anymore. You're supposing another world and assuming your form within it, whatever that might be. It's really an act of faith—to decide on at least one near-impossible thing every day, and believe it.

*

As the world has expanded from and beyond the marble size of school, what's become clearer is that I never told lies for myself. My lies were always for others, so that people might feel more comfortable in my company. I was, near constantly, preoccupied with my relationships. I table-hopped until Year 8 and its ultimatum: either settle into a friendship group, or have no friends. Until then, I hadn't really understood that other people, things you like, things you know about, can't make you solid. That breeze you call a sense of self? That's something you're gonna have to work on. It was really me versus object permanence every day—and I mean that in both the sincerely anxious and the quietly narcissistic sense.

I realised a few years ago that every knot I'm trying to untangle was formed between the ages of three and twelve. One fun knot is that I don't really like fruit—specifically apples, oranges, bananas and grapes. It's not for the taste or texture, but because of the memory of three boys in my Year 3 class (whose government names I will take to my grave) chewing up and spit-spraying fruit across the playground, entirely unprovoked. It's an imprint I don't think of often, but when I do, it's like the outlines of the other imprints rise to the surface: aversions or inclinations, tendencies to lean one way instead of the other, like deeply repressed muscle memory. So much of *then* steers who I am now, to the point where there's not actually a clear division.

I love to learn what people were like in school, equal parts for the information, and for all the different ways their faces change when asked the question. Often, when considering childhood, experiences are classed as either resolved or unresolved—not always cleanly, sometimes somewhere between the two—but in fact a trace would be truer, images over images, presents over pasts that are still kind of ongoing. Those first-feelings become embroiled with their new, exciting, more severe iterations. I see myself as a kid trying to handle things differently—I catch myself now trying to warn kid me away from choices I've already made, or even to steer myself away from paths and lines of thinking I went down years ago. In the 1991 Studio Ghibli deep cut *Only Yesterday* (a perfect film, without which this chapbook would not exist in its current form), the lead character, Taeko, recalls moments from when she was ten years old, memories rising up to the surface as she considers her life as a whole, who she is and what she wants. It's strange watching something and feeling like your mind is a projector, every sequence coming straight out of your own head.

*

The *fovea centralis* is a small depression that sits in the retina, right at the back of your eye, and is responsible for producing sharp, detailed vision. This was first explained to me during an anatomy lecture I mostly didn't under-stand. But I loved the way the words sounded and took to the symbol of it quite quickly. This little pit, purposed for light—not shade or dim or dark. It was gold I didn't have

4

to pan very hard for. I kept saying it, and saying it. People would ask me how uni was going, how I was doing, what I was reading, where the bathroom was—and I would open my mouth to tell them about an indent we all have in the backs of our eyes. It gave me something to cede to people who asked if I wrote poems about biomedical science: *Oh, no. But there is this one cool thing I just learned...*

To me, the *fovea* represents two things: aspirational acuity, and fundamental receptivity. I used to spend so long yearning for acuity, wanting to know precisely where my body started and ended, to be sharp and deliberate, to make myself solid, to do justice to that watery kid. In more recent years, as I have grown more substantial, my weight has shifted towards the receptivity part—the ability to sit still, open, ready, and with gratitude.

*

The poems in this book have come to be from journal entries and private blog posts, notebook and Notes app fragments, from workshops with Barbican Young Poets and Octavia Poetry Collective, from commutes, from many pensive meals alone in Tartine Artisanal on Tooting Broadway, from the foyers of the institutions that line the Southbank, from a cabin on the Isle of Wight that became the Isle of PoC for a weekend, from downstairs at the Curzon Bloomsbury, from half-hour lunch breaks during Sunday shifts at the suitcase store, from the minutes before and after lectures, from waiting at a bus stop for the 492 to Sidcup in the rain, from every train journey between Dartford and London Bridge, and from the Northern line, recording forty-five-minute voice notes to send back and forth across continents.

I hope the poems here read like an EP (s/o Banks and Mary for, on separate occasions, offering that analogy).

And speaking of life-long friends. This book would not exist in the way that it does without them, the loves of my life who care so generously, who drag me by the scruff of my neck and remind me that I'm alive! Right now! And now! And now! I write in awe of and in gratitude to them, how they have coaxed me out of myself, loving me and challenging me in one swift movement. Every poem is a part of the acknowledgements.

A while back, one of these fierce friends emailed:

I've learnt that the world can so quickly leave you behind if you don't force your way back into it.

The poems in this book are both an attempt to tell the truth of how things have gone for me, so far, and to stop getting left behind—distracted by things in the corner of my eye.

PLAYLIST

Mountain Man – 'Guilt'

Cécile McLorin Salvant – 'And Yet'

Kadhja Bonet – 'Remember the Rain'

Makaya McCraven feat. Brandee Younger, Tomeka Reid, Dezron Douglas & Joel Ross – 'Black Lion'

St. Vincent – 'Severed Crossed Fingers'

Monica Martin – 'Cruel'

Weaves – 'Help!'

Solange – 'Time (is)'

Denai Moore – 'Offer Me'

keiyaA – 'Hvnli'

Nick Hakim – 'CRUMPY'

Four Tet – 'Daughter'

Laura Mvula – 'Bread'

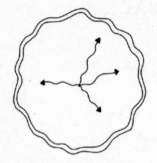

POETRY HAS
BROKEN THE BACK

poetry has broken the back of my voice
craft a bowl
from spine
like lifted hands
waiting for something to fall
into them
poetry is taping postcards
to hotel room walls, i'm dizzy
i'm watching a film in a language
i don't understand and
i'm watching my hands
write subtitles
i'm falling asleep on my phone
i'm speaking into my hands
i'm sweetening my tea
with baby teeth
i'm wringing out the last of a cold sweat
i'm lighting a candle at both ends
and the candle is me
and the waiting centre is me
and the glowing wicks are me

i'm alight

PRIMARY

A PIN THROUGH
THE FOLDED PAGE

I break the water's seal (teeth first, this time) and wade
to shore

where the sinewy girl in the green summer dress waits

playing a game I don't remember teaching her, compassing,
touching the tops of sorrow's many heads.

... duck, duck ...

I'm a welcome interruption.
Holding off the chase *is* the game, I realise.

She tells me I'm a swallow, and I keep slamming into her
bedroom window.

I tell her to stop sitting opposite me on the train—I can't
write when she does that.

*

She asks, *do you think we'll be able to feel it, when the spinning stops?*

a sitting duck now, combing the sand.

I say, *I think the skin on our backs will kiss the skin on our fronts*

and her fingers slack, and she rolls her eyes,
and she tells me, again, to stop treating her like a child.

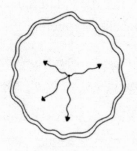

SCHOOL POEM
(IN THE PHOTO ABOVE MY PEG)

I wonder at the girl in the photo above my peg so much
that at playtime Miss follows me into the cloakroom.

I know the girl in the photo, I see her all the time
and all the time, she's doing something different.

Miss asks what she's doing now
and I keep my mouth closed

because I don't yet know how to say:
she runs, screaming, like her name out of your mouth.

operatic (*as in* needful)
like her name out of your mouth—

the girl runs from you like her name
out of your mouth, Miss.

You speak her like a blade
cut from lead, so she runs

unspooling across the frame and (from no place) back again
outline hanging from her, an unhemmed dress

she leaps, billowing, frame to frame, billowing, she leaps

she runs, so fast   you look back   and you look back

you look back   so fast   she runs, Miss.

AN ANGEL, LAUGHING
HERSELF OUT OF THE SKY

Dear God, I have something to tell you. I peeled a girl today, like she was an apple. She went bright red and her eyes bulged to hold the pain. You should have seen it.

She was upside down, hanging from the metal bars where Caleb fell and cracked his skull open last year. And because she wasn't there to see it, I had to tell her—about what would happen to her skull, the brilliant sound of her opening. How it's the same as when Kayleigh hits a rounders ball, clean and hard, and it vanishes in the sun's cold glare. How you can't come back from a crack like that. I told her all of this and she kept swinging, like I wasn't there. Goodness and Mercy must have abandoned me, God.

I wasn't mean. I just told everyone she was mean to me. And then, like a fuse, she went out. I even heard the small animal inside her hit the ground (as I write this, it must still be warm). She cried so hard that by last lesson, when I looked up, she wasn't there. She cried so hard, she emptied herself from the room. We disappeared her together. God, I've felled so many trees, but this was my first body. I wanted to laugh so badly.

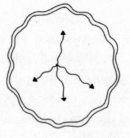

WOMAN

(after 'Suddenly Afraid' by Lydia Davis)

not to say there are some words I can't spell
not to say they were never meant for me
not to say I can't belong to them
not to say 'no place' is safer than 'some place'
not to strip anyone of a comfort but
maybe there are some words
I can't spell for a reason

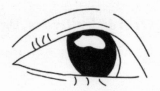

SCHOOL POEM
(FED)

and the spoon was in my mouth when I woke
and I didn't ask why
and maybe I should have, but instead I swallowed it
and the cool metal slid down my throat
and the silver was—at once—within me (like it was
never its own)
and I found that I could be fed by a tool for feeding
and I never hungered again

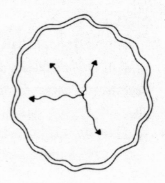

LIAM

All the boys I like are small—
smaller than me and small altogether.
Flighty. Smiles gummy and wide
as mid-July, full as major chords.

I watch Liam's calves as he runs.
He's new, so when the game starts,
asks why I'm not playing—
face so open I can hear him think.

Says, *I'll chase you.*
Splits the soft moment
and offers me the bigger half.
I feel my legs swing over the bench.

THREE GIRLS
(TALE)

Three girls with the same birthday—what can they do
but gather with their mothers and ask questions:

When, where, what time, and how long
they each were.

They quilt three stories together, the mothers seed
the threads and the daughters pull.

When it is done, braided,
they pitch a camp by the water.

The daughters notice for the first time
their mothers' webbed hands and feet.

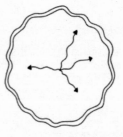

WHEN A STORY TELLS
ITSELF TO STOP

tell it it's pretty, a joke to break the ice
                            smear blush on its cheeks

corkscrew a hole in its side
                            make something of the entrails

a rivulet to coax out the river
                            though it won't wind the same

soak it in warm water
                            run its mother's hands over its sore

arc, like a hymn
            yes, call it a hymn

take it somewhere to cool down
            check the switches and replace the bulbs

tell it its sister asks of it every night
needs it to kill something in the corner of her room.

SUNFLOWER / SAFFLOWER

We're in the greenhouse at the far end of the field
heaving from the sprint, sticking to ourselves, pointing
to the same plot.
Look, sunflower, you say.
Look, safflower, I say—
rows of yellow that couldn't be
believed to bleed the way they eventually do.
Some things are so unsightly, they become sad.
Things like children leaving the faith they were raised with
or puddles in the heat.

I want to cut your eyelashes
so they grow in thistled like mine
and we both have to pare things away to see.
See how the truth starts as a seed or a stone?
How you can't make one the other?
I want to rub this truth against the roof of your mouth.
Once it's under the tongue, once it's against the gums
there is no going back, I'm afraid.
You're the first person I spoil, in this way.

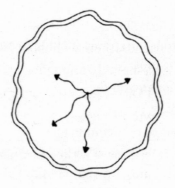

SCHOOL POEM
(SPILLED WARM)

If we were friends, there would not have been a leash.
All of us dense-boned, trampoline-skinned—we would
have knocked knees, danced together, mimetic
—look at Newton's cradle!

It would not have always been me, outside and uncollared,
prizeless as I am. It would not have always been
my coins, for your slots. Now, I know.

Now, I want all of the people who made me feel
(because they knew they could make me feel)
to feel what I make them.

I want the girls who stood on toilet seats and towered
over my stall to have the backs of *their* legs
turn cold, run down by their own spilled warm too.

WHEN I GET MY DEGREE
IN MARRYING WELL

my mother will have finished weaving the stems of
days together. place the wreath, verdant and outsize,
around my neck.

she'll say, *my baby, my rondo, oh my figure of 1!*
and i'll kiss her, the heads of spared flowers
between my lips.

o, she will smile! with teeth! promising
to ruin anyone who tries to ruin me.

and i'll sift myself then, and she won't notice
—eyes closed so tight, she'll have fireworks.

AGAIN,

AGAIN

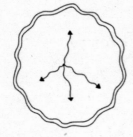

LANGUAGE

(a duplex, after Jericho Brown)

A language, like blood, takes two people to let,
It's a dress I can't unzip on my own.

      My life, sometimes, unzips on its own.
      One mutinous nail against the length of a rib.

Anything can be deboned starting from a rib.
Twenty-four deft pulses and I open out,

      alive. The year makes whole months open out.
      The card I draw from the deck is Temperance.

Face down—still, the card I draw is Temperance.
Cheek to my mother's back, tied by a wrapper.

      What is language if not tying a wrapper?
      A weight to hold your body upright,

a child splinting both our bodies upright.
A language, like blood, takes two people to let.

SELF-PORTRAIT AS
EIGHT-TRACK MIX
(JUNE 2019)

1.

I imagine as many Frank Oceans as there are harmonies on Frank Ocean's rendition of 'Moon River'. One, spotlight centre. Another behind, head resting on his shoulder. One sat, one lying on his side, one running full speed, one crawling, belly to the floor. Three walking in step, swinging their legs in lines across one another. One on a sailboat, anchored, miles away. One in the room above this one, pacing a slowly drawn circle. A Frank Ocean cuts through a red sheet, calls the slit vibrato. I cross the river with both hands to my chest.

2.

Mitski sings 'Humpty' and apologises. You gave her a nursery rhyme and she broke it, made it a sorrow song. Her cold palms slam again again at the keys of the piano, at the skin of the drums, like buoys on the waves of her voice. The room is not steady. I tell her, today, eggshells are too frail for me to touch as well.

Where is Paolo Nutini?

3.
Someone describes Monica Martin's voice as 'like glass'. So clear you see straight through it with a sliver of yourself out there too. Think: mountain, cabin, window, winter, glass. And you can see the frost on the tips of everything outside, and that slightly angled reconstruction of yourself in it too. Like you're somehow also outside in the cold—that's her voice. Her voice puts you on the other side of glass, splits you, which I think is too masterful an act to call reflection.

Where did he go? Sauntering, with that voice

4. / 5.
Bedouine and José González are doing some kind of dance—clapping, and circling each other—like flamenco. They are at the hearth, fanning the low flames, warming from somewhere deep. Their lips barely move. They sing like ventriloquists.

Mug of tea in his hand, with that voice

6.
Oh, Twigs? Twigs is spinning. So fast you think she's four-dimensional, like her face goes the whole way around. You see all of her at once and your mind makes sense of it.

7.

Paolo is found two-stepping around someone else's living room. Remembers that time he got Janelle Monáe on a track and tries tightroping across the carpet. Does so perfectly. His laugh is a kind half-cackle, forty years older than him. It's what people mean when they say 'salt of the earth'.

8.

Aminé brings his mum wherever he goes. On the hook, in the ad libs—*Hey!* he says to her. He wears home like a smile because both are both. Out on the field, he's all nerves, either throwing fakes or bailing from a receive. We're on the same team: him, me, and those piles of mashed-up soft tissue from *Stranger Things*—us people that wear our insides on our out.

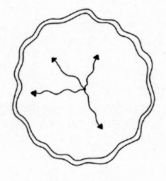

CRUSHING
(IN SIX PARTS)

i
After one day at your side
I lie down on my front
and am broken.

ii
Love. If you can get past the smell of it, the taste is
pretty good.
And then you walk, following it like a season, like spring,
like bees tapping against an east-facing window,
like running from rains that are yet to come.

iii
You ask me to come as I am,
to enter your room ungilded, unshimmering.
We meet eye to eye
breathing each other's breath
because—you say—it's not a kiss unless our lips touch.

iv

For you, I hold my heart in my hands
[a wet fish, muscling its way from my grip].
What could it be to make a heart of paper and wax?
Dripping and drying and leaving itself on people
and things—is this it?

v

Now, my arms, low and outstretched before me,
plead with the empty theatre, implore
the empty seats for a stem—no flower, even.

vi

You made me feel as though I was allergic to air.
Take shallow breaths.
I wake up and still
my dreams are only rumours.

BIRTHDAY

One year, instead of cutting the cake

>   face screwed into a pucker, chewed into
>   sugary nothing

Instead of looping the silk bow, amber

>   between my back and its brace

I become the cake, with a knife inside

>   delicious and inscrutable

like groundwater belting beneath the soil

>   confounding the dowser, with a knife inside

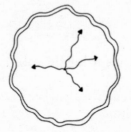

WAY OUT
(TALE)

we're way out in the wilderness now
(way, way out)

and our soles have never been this hot
(like a sound and a colour and a smell)

and our palms have been made to open
(slow, like the word 'wound')

by the bark, by the climbing
(by the cold, by its appetite)

and what will we do? when it gets real bad
(and our hands can't hold any longer)

one of us says: i guess we amputate, at least they aren't
the parts we need to—
one of us walks off, one of us says

well, what happens then? what happens when it's
our throats?
(the hunter diffused into the air around us)

what happens when it's our friends?
(and we can no longer sound the low threat of a swarm)

what happens when—

neatly then, the soreness calls for us
(a dart to the neck)

we hang our young,
high up on the branches

we find a cove, we tighten into it
we sleep like a pile and we sleep like a hole in the ground

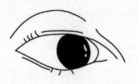

IT'S NOT LIKE I'M A HOUSE
FULL OF MIRRORS

but I am a House of Mirrors, a contract of play
so the mirrors keep their mouths open

wide with no sound because there is no one there
to hear it, whisperscream *i love you i love you i love you*

fall into one another, collapse and collapse saying
i love you i love you i love y— until someone walks in

and even if there's dirt on your shoes, even if
your skin cells go, when you go, they go with you

some people write words in permanent marker
some people stick chewing gum to the floor

some people lick the walls
but all of it goes with them when they go

funny no one ever brings a blowtorch
or a hammer or a spade

some people have left bodies here, and still
when they go, they go with them

some people take photos, and when they develop
the background is the place they have felt most at home

and they believe the House of Mirrors
is the place they have felt most at home

it wouldn't be tiring to be a house full of mirrors
but it's tiring to be a House of Mirrors

for it to be your very architecture, and it's sad
to know you once had hands to make yourself this way

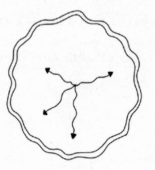

AFTER THE READING

(after 'Poem for My Love' by June Jordan)

> *How do we come to be here next to each other*
> *in the night*
> *Where are the stars that show us to our love*
> *inevitable*

after the reading, or the debrief, or the *in conversation*
when it is summer, and by some juicy miracle
we are all still unbruised, dangling from our branches

near bursting our own flesh, we bottleneck the doorway
and baptise the street—abandon the day's serious feeling
after the reading, or the debrief, or the *in conversation*

because despite being born into the slick arms of alienation
we are all still unbruised, dangling from our branches
without memory of a time 'when outside was safe'

put simply, when you realise you are only a lapse of time
long enough to be given a name, there is no use in
thinking of 'capacity' or 'tomorrow'
after the reading, or the debrief, or the *in conversation*

one House Red forgets you your watch. you mumble

something like, *isn't it wild how babies hiccup in the womb? isn't that sad?*

we are all still unbruised, dangling from our branches

black and plural under a coral sky

we circle back to the topic of us—wanting everything

after the reading, or the debrief, or the *in conversation*

BARFLIES

The barflies dance to the bottom of their glass—giddy, and full—walking home with eyes glazed ruby red, conjoined, sharing a single socket. Every shop on the main road is closed. The shutters are even half down on the Romanian grocers. The barflies slow—catch two pairs of legs swaying in the aisles, twining under the sterile light. One pair of hands around a waist. Footsteps perfect on tiles. Sarah Vaughan's 'Lullaby of Birdland' scales the air that escapes from under the shutters. Two birds lifting off a moonlit lake.

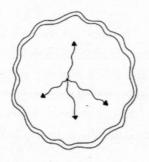

BODY LOCKED IN AIR

strange how she moves / mostly / one alert muscle
single unit / crown to toe / snout to tail / carving into
the world / arcing or nothing / two settings / ready and
waiting / statue within boulder / precise / holding down
pause button / every breath / in conversation / cut out
during rehearsal / lines in the mirror / both parts / just
in / case.

oh— / she says / it's a balance / left by her mother
a woman / so good / at getting up / she does it / in her
sleep.

PARTINGS

It takes me forever to say goodbye to people I meet in living rooms, or queues.

I tell the intern at the exhibition to take care of herself four times.

I give my phone number to the woman who helps me up off the floor, my skateboard wheels spinning in the air.

I thank the girl with the bleached eyebrows *so much* for watching my bags.

I thank her for so long, even the servers start looking at me funny.

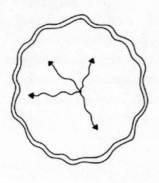

I TELL TIME

last year, i decide to split this year up. take Time into my untamed hands. i mention this to Time over the phone, think i send her a voice note, like: *all you're gonna feel next year, yeah, are my hands around your neck!* Time has the darkest jokes though, because this year is now actually made up of stretches of time marked by the loss of a ring. i ended this last stretch without a jewel blue one. i tell Time, this is fine. this is fine because—actually—my mother wears the first and only real ring ever made. i tell Time, you know at first i thought, wow. what a horror, for that ring, to be bound. what loneliness it must feel. but then, then i grew up, and realised, of course it's not lonely, it has her. a person and her ring are like a flag and its territory. no, like a flag and its pole. no, like a flag and its wind. sometimes the wind changes (is in a foul, clouding mood) and the flag tangles, slaps against the pole, tears at a seam. but then (then) like clockwork, the wind remembers its promise. the flag is back to billowing, happy to be whatever colour it might be so long as its hands thrust toward, against, around the neck of its beautiful companion. or actually, maybe it's not like a flag and its wind, i tell Time, maybe it's more like a gut and its swallow. *duh*, Time says, *that's the joke?*

so, i keep buying rings and i keep losing them. i tell Time, you know, my mum wears gold and i wear silver, but the main difference between us is i keep losing rings. i think it's because she's a sun in herself, so each atom in the metal feels light by her, and i'm the moon, because i'm so concerned with revolution i can't see straight! i just want to be that kind of heat, i tell Time, a degree only the centre of a sun could hit. i want to be hot and impressive, so a hot ring wants to press, to impress, me too. and it's because i'm always thinking about it that it never happens. i turn things over in my hands a lot. i turn things over in my hands and they go cold. sometimes, i think i get it from my dad. something like how he prayer-beads his words under cold water for hours before opening up my palm, setting them down gently. we're two sides of the same. he's like, when you pull a shoelace and the knot tightens, and i'm like when it falls apart. i remember in p.e. we learned that tall people slouch because we have a low centre of gravity, and that means we have weaker cores, and so, we just, slowly... stop texting back? start thinking *god! please! just! clap me like a mosquito and end it already.* and then, when it gets real bad, we just let our centres sigh, and bend our bodies up into little black holes.   it happened to me.

it wasn't even that dark though, little bits of light kept coming in. imagine that, i tell Time, sometimes you think you've finally made a little black hole you can call your own, you think, *finally*, you're on a train, and you're going through that long tunnel. and then, you open your eyes. they were just closed the whole time. they just... closed the whole time. i don't want to split

74

my year up, not really. i would like to put Time on and wear it through my day, not turn it over in my hands. the more i play with it the more likely i am to lose it. my mum said that to me once.

RAFT

The last week of September, Miriam makes a meal.
The garden doors are open, she is aproned.
I busy myself with the performance of tending to her
(lending no skill whatsoever).

I tell her, every once in a while I'll just need to push
my raft off the shore, steal away
and sail along for a while before washing up
leaner and more alive.

I'll always wash up after a few days.

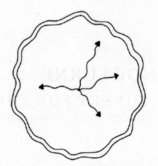

NOCTURNE
(SONNET FOR THE SOUTHEASTERN)

On the train my body drops an octave
(becomes the colour of a candle's fire
the night will press out with two licked fingers)
and the 'ACAB' on the new build between
Lewisham and London Bridge is a trip switch
so the Southeastern is not a vehicle
but a portal to Elete and the bar
she will be dancing on in an hour
all orange pleather *go-go!* centrepiece
and the body will not be an instrument
but a measure, close to time if time could
ever move like that, without an axis.
All praise the bouquet of us in the night
fresh cut, and only as old as we are.

ACKNOWLEDGEMENTS

Thank you to my parents, my brother and my baby sister for making the matter of me, for your care and protection, for keeping me upright.

Thank you to the great loves of my life, to those who have cast your eyes over these poems, given them your thoughts in emails and voice notes. To those of you who have made this life worth living. To Elete N-F. Thank you for being my very first wife, for sheltering me, for remembering everything, for talking me down from various ledges, and for always being there. To Miriam Gauntlett, whose friendship is a lesson in consistency, generosity and heart. Thank you for your fierce care, and for never, not once, holding it back. To Lola Olufemi, for challenging me, and for teaching me how to spell enjoyment—for dragging me out of my head and into the club. Thank you for taking what I name as complicated and showing me how it might be simple. To Victoria Adukwei Bulley—I simply would not be the poet I am if not for you, V. Thank you for your care, as a writer and a friend. To Hareem Ghani, for plucking me out of isolation and into a movement—thank you for cussing me out and keeping me humble. To Banks Alo, what do I even say! Thank you for letting me talk at you for hours, for taking your time and being deliberate, and for showing me what being a multi-hyphenate really looks like. Thank you to my whole wayward family—Sandy Ogundele, Christine Pungong, Fope Olaleye, Audrey Sebatindira, Hannah Dualeh, Shahla Omar, Mahamed Abdullahi. Thank you to my wolfpack, my day 1s—Mary Odonkor, Zahra Lee, Shannon Harris, Emily Wilcox and Caitlin Moore. Thank you to Ankita Saxena for grounding me in the middle of assembling these poems—your warmth means so much.

Thank you to my BYP family—to Jacob Sam-La Rose, for being a first-teacher to me and to countless others, and for showing me what poetry makes possible. Thank you to my Octavia sisters—to Rachel Long for building that world-making space, for every workshop, and for every pre- and post-workshop chat, wandering out of the Southbank.

Thank you to everyone who has ever asked me to read a poem.

Thank you to Farhaana and Brekhna, for making all of this possible.

*

The poem 'Woman' is written after Lydia Davis' short story 'Suddenly Afraid'.

'Language' is written as a duplex, a form invented by Jericho Brown.

'After the reading' is written after June Jordan's 'Poem for My Love', a short extract of which is reprinted here with gratitude to the June M. Jordan Literary Estate Trust.